SECULAR

SSAA, body percussion, and spoons

Marie Madeleine

Trad. Acadian

arr. Jeanette Gallant

MUSIC DEPARTMENT

OXFORD
UNIVERSITY PRESS

Marie Madeleine

Marie Madeleine ton p'tit jupon de laine,	*Mary Madeleine your little woollen petticoa*
ta p'tite jupe carreautée, ton p'tit jupon piqué.	*your little checkered skirt, your little fitted petticoa*
Mon père avait une p'tite vache noire.	*My father had a little black cow*
Ell' donnait yin que du lait caillé.	*She gave nothing but sour milk*
Elle cherchait yin qu'à m'en corner.	*She wanted nothing but to corner me*
J'étais obligé de l'attacher.	*I was obliged to tie her up*
Un jour son câbl'il a cassé.	*One day her cable broke*
La vache m'a envoyé revoler.	*The cow sent me flying*
La vache m'a envoyé revoler.	*The cow sent me flying*
À plat ventre sur le tas d'fumier.	*Lying on a heap of manure*
J'étais beau quand je m'suis relevé.	*I was sightly when I got up*
Ça a pris trois jours pour m'nettoyer.	*It took three days to get clean*

Trad. Acadia

This is an arrangement of an Acadian folksong entitled *Marie Madeleine*, more commonly classified in th French-Canadian folksong repertoire as 'Une petite vache noire'. This short, lively piece is loads of fun and highligh the quintessential elements of the Acadian folksong tradition: podorythmie (seated foot-tapping), diddlag (mouth music), and the spoons[1]. A challenging and complex piece, it reflects the innate musicality c this long-standing Canadian oral tradition while stretching the tradition to include more modern elements.

The Acadians are a French-speaking diasporic community who largely live in Canada's east coast provinces. Durin colonial times, the Acadians endured a series of deportations by the English in small groups from Canada beginning i 1755. Though many returned after a seven-year exile, some Acadians found a new home, including those who are th ancestors of the Cajuns in Louisiana.

Although this folksong can be found in other parts of French Canada, I chose to feature the Acadian dialect in th rendition because it is emblematic of the role that language plays in creating social inequity. Acadian writer an historian, George Arsenault, generously helped me to include various elements of the Acadian dialect such as th phrase 'yin que' (which has the same meaning as 'rien que' in standardized French). Due to their colonial past, th Acadians have a different sense of history and linguistic identity to that of Canada's larger French population, th Québécois. This piece shines a light on the social and linguistic stratification of the Acadians who—up until mor recent years—were thought to be 'lesser' in social status than other Canadians.

This song is part of my family story. It often was sung by my father, my Auntie Lily, and my Uncle Richard, a Acadians who suffered the impacts of these historic wrongs. My father, Paul Gallant (1917–2008), was the youngest c ten children and had a grade eight education. He was the lucky one; most of my Acadian aunts and uncles could nc read or write. Folksong would remain the only remnant of my father's Acadian past because he not only had to lose hi French accent to find work, but was told by a nun from Québec to stop speaking the Acadian dialect at home because was a 'low class' form of French. I dedicate this arrangement to my father's memory with love.

Jeanette Gallan

[1] Please note that I have modified the rhythm of the basic step (pas de base) of the podorythmie used in Acadian reels. Rather than writing ♫♩♫♩ I have written the rhythm as ♫♩ ♫♩ because it fit better with the clapping and spoon percussion patterns written for this arrangement. This son also is traditionally categorized as an 'enumerative' folksong where the last phrase of a verse is used to start the next verse. To tell the story mor efficiently in this modern era, I have only included key verses which advance the story more quickly.

Pronunciation guides, a studio recording, and a learning video for the body percussion are available through the companion website at *www.oup.com/marie_madeleine*

Marie Madeleine

Traditional Acadian French folksong
arr. JEANETTE GALLANT

* 'dum' is pronounced with an 'ah' vowel

At the director's discretion, choirs may begin with an introduction of clapping and seated foot-tapping (perhaps using bars 10–17 in the score, and stopping on the first beat of bar 17) before the voices enter.

Duration: 3 mins

Printed in Great Britain

OXFORD UNIVERSITY PRESS, MUSIC DEPARTMENT, GREAT CLARENDON STREET, OXFORD OX2 6DP

4

* In the seated foot-tapping (podorythmie), the right foot moves forward (F) then back (B).

* Note the down and up strokes of the spoon pattern beginning in bar 62.

† Sing on 'm'.

13

101 **a tempo**
CLAPPING

SEATED-FOOT TAPPING

mf ... *p* ——— *mp*
Ça a pris trois jours pour m'net - to - yer. Ma - rie!

mf ... *p* ——— *mp*
Ça a pris trois jours pour m'net - to - yer. Ma - rie!

mf
Ça a pris trois jours pour m'net - to - yer. Ma - de-leine ton

mf ... *mp*
Ça a pris trois jours pour m'net - to - yer. *did - dle dum dum di dum dum*

a tempo
mf
mp

105

p ——— *mp*
Ma - rie!

p ——— *mp*
Ma - rie!

p'tit ju-pon de laine, ta p'tite jupe car-reau-tée, ton p'tit ju-pon pi-qué. Ma-de-leine ton

did - dle did - dle dum did - dle dum di dum dum did - dle did - dle dum dum di dum dum

W217 **Marie Madeleine (SSAA)** GALLANT

OXFORD
UNIVERSITY PRESS

www.oup.com

ISBN 978-0-19-354375-1

9 780193 543751